The
World's Best
Doctor Jokes

The World's Best Doctor Jokes

Dr. Raja Korale

Illustrations by Quentin

Fontana
An Imprint of HarperCollinsPublishers

Fontana
An Imprint of HarperCollins*Publishers,*
77–85 Fulham Palace Road,
Hammersmith, London W6 8JB

Published by Fontana 1991
9 8 7 6 5 4 3 2

First published by the author in a limited
edition as *Laughter is the Best Medicine*
This edition first published by Angus & Robertson 1984
(reprinted nine times)

ISBN 0 00 638075 1

Set in Baskerville

Printed in Great Britain by
HarperCollinsManufacturing Glasgow

Then there was the theatre sister who was known among her colleagues as "The Appendix" . . . because every surgeon took her out.

*   *   *

Heard in the theatre during a D & C (Dilatation and Curette) operation . . .
Gynaecologist: "At your cervix Madam".
Patient: "I am dilated to meet you".

*   *   *

Two psychiatrists bumped into each other in the Consultant's lounge.
"How am I feeling?" said the first.
"Fine, fine, you're feeling fine. How am I feeling?" replied the second.

An old lady went to the doctor complaining of swollen ankles. After giving her a thorough examination he reassured her:

"It's only a bit of fluid. There is nothing to worry about. I'll give you some water tablets. Just take one every alternate day and see me in a fortnight".

"I am not quite with you doctor. Can you explain how to take the tablets".

"Oh, its quite simple. Take the first one this morning, skip tomorrow, take another day after tomorrow and skip the next day and go on doing that until you see me again".

When the patient came back two weeks later her ankles had gone down completely.

"Well it's marvellous" said the doctor, there is no swelling at all. You don't have to take any more tablets".

"Thank God for that" said the old lady "the SKIPPING was killing me".

*   *   *

Then there was the case of the young girl who had the itch between her toes . . . er . . . the big ones.

A woman swallowed a fifty-pence piece and went to see her doctor about it.

The doctor told her: "There is no need to worry, Miss Dawson. I will give you some opening medicine. Keep a look out for it when your bowels move".

A few day later, she went back to the surgery.

"Ah yes, Miss Dawson. Have you passed that coin?"

Miss Dawson didn't look too pleased. "Doctor, I haven't passed the 50p coin, but I have passed three 10p coins", she said.

The GP thought for a while, then said: "How old are you, Miss Dawson?"

"I'll be 45 in September".

"I've got it now", said the doctor "it's the CHANGE!"

*　　　　*　　　　*

Then there was the ENT surgeon who was such a well known homosexual that he was called "The QUEER nose and Throat Specialist".

A man goes to the doctor: "I've been feeling a little off colour lately".

"Well what have you been eating recently?" asked the doctor.

"I only eat Billiard Balls".

"Billiard Balls???".

"Yes, blue ones for breakfast, a pink and lightly salted yellow for lunch, reds for snacks, and for dinner a brown, another blue and a well roasted black".

"Aha", said the doctor. "I see what the trouble is — you've been skipping your greens".

*   *   *

Major Pectoralis met Miss Labia Majora in the supermarket.

"Hello! Majora. How are you keeping?"

"Very well, thank you. How's life with you?"

"Can't grumble. Oh! By the way I haven't seen your sister for a long time".

"You mean Minora? She rarely comes out".

*   *   *

Then there was the truck driver who stopped to AVOID a child . . . and fell off the bed.

The well known Professor of Rectal Surgery was on his ward rounds, with his usual retinue of junior doctors, sister, registrar, medical students, nurses, etc.

When he came to the last bed, the patient pointed out to the sister that the Professor had something behind his right ear.

The sister then whispered to the great man — "Sir, you have a suppository behind your right ear".

"You know what it means, sister!" — shouted the grand old Professor — "Some bum's got my pencil!"

*　　　　　*　　　　　*

This old professor was going on and on about the anatomy and physiology of the male genitalia. It was getting rather embarrassing for the female medical students.

He went on "the Bantu tribe in Southern Africa is known to have the longest . . ."

One girl at the back of the lecture theatre decided that she had had enough and walked out.

You could hear a pin drop as she walked to the door.

When she had reached the door the Professor said.

"There is no hurry madam. The next plane to Southern Africa leaves London Heathrow at 9.30am on Saturday morning".

Doctor . . . "Have you ever been incontinent?"
Patient . . . "No, I've only been to Blackpool".

* * *

In a remote village hospital in Africa, one of the natives had to have one of his testicles removed following a road traffic accident. It was the usual practice to have a plastic prosthetic sutured — in, for cosmetic reasons.
Unfortunately, on that day they were "out of stock".
The only thing the Theatre Sister could come up with was an onion to match the same size.
A month later, when the patient was seen in the Outpatients' Clinic, the surgeon asked him "Any problems?"
"None at all doctor. The wound has healed up nicely. However, sometimes when I scratch down below my eyes start watering".

* * *

Heard in UTERO . . .
1st TWIN to 2nd TWIN . . . "Oh, shut up. DAD'S coming in".

Patient: "Doctor, I've been feeling terrible all week".
Doctor: "Well, get undressed and I'll examine you".
Doctor . . . (20 minutes later) . . . "Sorry, — I can't find anything wrong with you. It must be the beer".
Patient: "OK — I'll come back when you're sober".

*   *   *

YOUR ABSENCE CONFIRMED YOU ARE AS EXPENDABLE AS YOUR APPENDIX, DAVIES...

The Casualty Sister was trying to sell a raffle ticket to the half-drunk patient.

"Sister, what is the raffle for", he asked.

She said "You see, one of our porters died last week. It is for his poor widow and three children".

He replied "No, No thank you Sister. I don't want any tickets. What would I do with a widow and three children? I've already got one woman and six children at home".

* * *

Then there was the bright fellow who said thiamine difficiency causes dermatitis over parts exposed to SIN.

*   *   *

A man went to the doctor with a very personal problem. He told his doctor that he had several holes in his "urinal" "Doctor it is very embarrassing. When I pass water, it comes out of all the holes and splashes around. It makes my clothes wet every time. It is even more embarrassing when I have to use a public toilet. It splashes around on the people who are standing nearby. Is there anything you can do to help me?"

The doctor thought for a while . . .

"I'll give you a letter to take to my brother" he said.

"Is he a good plastic surgeon?" asked the patient hopefully.

"Oh No! He is a musician. He plays the trombone for a jazz band. I'll ask him to give you a few lessons".

*   *   *

Remember . . . "Prevention is better than curette".
"Contraception is better than termination".

A young man went to see his doctor because he had a bald patch. His doctor had a casual look at it and said: "Oh, it's only a touch of alopecia. I'll give you an ointment and a shampoo".

"Doctor, before I came on your panel, my previous doctor sent me to the skin hospital. They've given me all the creams and ointments under the sun. They even tried ultra violet rays. There is no improvement at all".

"In that case young man, there is nothing I can give you. However, I can suggest a few methods which you can try.

ONE   You can have a hair transplant which is going to cost you a lot of money.

TWO   You can try accupuncture which may or may not work. Again it is going to cost you a fair bit.

THIRDLY There is an inexpensive method which I know has worked wonders in many cases".

"What is that method, doctor?"

"Applying female secretions on the bald patch".

"Very well, doctor, I think I'll give it a try. Thank you very much".

As he was leaving the surgery the patient noticed that the doctor was himself quite bald.

"Excuse me, doctor, but I notice that you are quite bald yourself".

"You are quite right, young man, but you would have also noticed that I have one hell of a moustache!"

Two homosexual spiders kept getting at each other's flies.

*   *   *

A woman swallowed a razor blade by accident. She went to her doctor who said: "Not to worry. We'll leave it alone and see what happens".

A few months later, when she eventually passed the razor blade, not only had she given herself a tonsillectomy, an appendicetomy and a hysterectomy, but had also castrated her husband, circumcised his best friend, given the Vicar a hare lip, and *still had a few shaves left* . . .

*   *   *

A middle aged man was told by his doctor to go to the eye hospital to have his eyes tested. He went in through a couple of doors when he saw a young nurse adjusting her underskirt.

"Nurse, my doctor said that I need to have my eyes tested".

"He's quite right" screamed the nurse, "this is the ladies!"

Doctor: "Are you troubled by improper thoughts?"
Patient: "No, I rather enjoy them".

*   *   *

"HE RAN OUT OF PATIENCE!"

An Indian lady doctor was trying her best to explain the withdrawal method of family planning to a Scottish gentleman. After a long time it finally dawned on him.

"I've got it now doctor. You mean like getting on the express train to Edinburgh and getting off at Preston".

*　　　　*　　　　*

Then there was the Manchester medical student who believed that St Luke was the Patron Siant of Lukoria (white discharge), Lukoderma (white patches on the skin) and Lukemia (disease of the white blood cells). The venereal diseases *clinic* in Manchester is named after Saint Luke who was a Physician.

*　　　　*　　　　*

The young nurse informed the patient: "Mr Jones you've only got three minutes to live".

"Nurse, is there anything you can do for me?"

"I am sorry Mr Jones, there isn't much I can do. Perhaps, I could boil an egg".

In a psychiatric ward two patients were discussing the news headlines. "Did you know that in New York one woman is knocked down by a car every three minutes".

"Poor woman, she must be in pretty bad shape".

*   *   *

Patient: "I hope I am ill, doctor".
Doctor: "What do you mean — you hope you are ill?"
Patient: "Well — I'd hate to be well and feel like this!"

*   *   *

When the contraceptive sheath first came out in America, this Irish girl wrote to her American pen pal.

"I hear you've got this wonderful new thing called the contraceptive. What exactly is a contraceptive?"

Her friend wrote back: "A contraceptive is something the Americans use at every conceivable moment".

"Doctor, have you anything for flat feet?"
"Yes — a foot pump!"

*　　　　　*　　　　　*

Did you hear the one about the man who kept returning to the Family Planning Clinic asking for a shorter sheath. Finally the doctor asked him: "Why what's wrong with the ones we have given you?"
"Oh! it is a bloody nuisance. They are too long. Every time I have to cut the end off!"

*　　　　　*　　　　　*

Last words of a virgin: "A little danger is a learning thing".

King and Queen were walking around the Palace gardens when they saw the Head Gardener's wife surrounded by six or seven kids.

"Are they all yours?" asked the Queen.

"Yes your Majesty, Robert has ten more at home".

"My God!" said the King "He should be given a Knighthood".

"He has one your Majesty, the trouble is he never uses it".

*   *   *

Spouse of a pretty young thing,
came home from war in the spring.
He was lame, but he came
with his hand on his cane,
A discharge is a wonderful thing.

*   *   *

There was a young lady named Twilling
Who went to her dentist for drilling
Because of depravity
He filled the wrong cavity
And now Twilling's nursing her filling.

In Czechoslovakia, a termination (an abortion) is known as a CROSSED CHEQUE.

*   *   *

A GYNAECOLOGIST is a man who works and operates in another man's FIELD.

*   *   *

Most experts are of the opinion that breast feeding has the definite advantage over bottle feeding. However, here are some of the less known advantages of breast feeding: —

1. It is always fresh
2. Readily available
3. The cat can't get at it
4. You don't have to shop around
5. Dad likes it too
6. Comes in handy containers
7. You don't have to leave the empties out for the milkman

Most experts however, fail to point out that you have to live with the containers.

*   *   *

The gynaecologist was in the theatre, doing his "list".

The surgeon, who had just finished an emergency operation in the adjoining theatre, popped his head through the door and said: "How's life, Bill?"

"Hello, Jim, just SCRAPING A LIVING".

The gynaecologist was just doing another termination!

In a remote African village, an albino child was born to one of the many wives of the Chief. The Chief was very angry and straight away he went to see the Christian Priest who was the only white man for hundreds of miles. He tried to explain to the Chief how an albino child comes about. But the Chief was not having any of his genetics.

Just then the Priest noticed some sheep grazing in a nearby field and to emphasise his point he showed him the only black sheep in the field among hundreds of white ones.

"OK! OK!" said the black chief.

"I no tell, you no tell!"

*   *   *

"Doctor, can you come round and see my wife as soon as possible? She is so ill that I had to carry her downstairs to make my breakfast".

*   *   *

Hear about the two peculiar judges?
They tried each other.

A psychiatrist asked a soldier during a medical test:
"What would happen if I cut off your ear?"

"I won't hear", answered the soldier.

"And if I cut off your other ear?"

"I won't see", replied he promptly.

"Why?"

"Because my cap would fall over my eyes", the soldier answered.

*　　　*　　　*

"What would be the first thing you would do if you had hydrophobia?" asked one teacher to another.

"I'd ask for a pencil and some paper".

"To make your last will?"

"No", replied the other wearily, "to make a list of the people I want to bite".

A masculine girl from Khartoum
Asked a ladylike boy to her room
They spent the whole night
In a hell of a fight
As to which should do what, and to whom.

*   *   *

"Doctor, can you give me something for my hands — they are shaking all the time".
"Do you drink a lot?"
"No doctor I spill most of it".

*   *   *

A bronchitic patient was given a prescription for some Aminophylline suppositories to help his breathing.
The doctor didn't explain to him how to use them.
The old man took the prescription to the chemist who duly dispensed them labelled "one daily as directed".
A few days later the patient went back to the chemist.
"Can you give me anything for my breathing? You know those tablets the doctor gave me last week, they were no use at all. For all the good they were, I might as well have stuck them up by back side".

"I COULD HAVE *SWORN* SOMEBODY CALLED 'SHOP!'"

Patient (at lunatic asylum):

"We like you better than the last Doctor".

"New Doctor" (flattered), "How is that".

"You seem more like one of us".

*   *   *

The medical director of a firm was baffled by an employee who kept asking for days off each time on the excuse that his wife had a childbirth.

The worker's first and second requests were granted without question, although they were only a few weeks apart.

But when, a fortnight later, he came in with the same story the doctor took him to task.

"How is it possible", he asked pointedly, "for your wife to have three childbirths in six weeks?"

"She is a midwife", was the reply. "Whenever she goes out on a job, I have to stay home and take care of the kids".

"...AND IF THESE PILLS DON'T CURE THE KLEPTOMANIA, TRY AND GET ME A VIDEO-RECORDER"

During the 2nd World war a doctor serving with the Allied forces wrote to his wife. She tried all morning to read his letter but was not very successful in deciphering what he had written. In desperation, longing to read every word her beloved husband had written she took the letter round to the friendly chemist in the neighbourhood. The chemist wasn't in a good mood and was about to go for his lunch. "Won't be a moment madam" he said taking the letter from her hand and rushing inside.

In three minutes flat he came back and handed over a bottle of cough mixture and a jar of ointment.

*　　　　*　　　　*

There was a young maid from Madras
Who had a magnificent ass:
Not pretty and pink,
As you probably think —
It was grey, had long ears, and ate grass!

*　　　　*　　　　*

Have you heard about the medical student who recently bought himself an electric "raiser".

A clever commercial female
Had prices tattooed on her tail;
And below her behind,
For the sake of the blind,
A duplicate version in Braille!

*　　　　*　　　　*

A doctor at a party was complaining bitterly to a lawyer friend . . . "Every time I mention to someone that I am a doctor they start reciting their symptoms and ask my opinion on whether their own doctors are treating them correctly. Do you have this problem, and how do you deal with it?"

"When I get home", said the lawyer, "I send them bills straight away — To:- Consultation at the party last night, £25 — that soon stops it".

"Jolly good idea", said the doctor, "I will do that".

Next morning he opened his mail, and the first letter was a bill from his lawyer friend — To:- Consultation at the party last night — £25".

The Taj Mahal is known as man's greatest erection for a woman.

*   *   *

A very obese man was having great difficulty trying to lose weight. His doctor tried him on all sorts of diets and slimming tablets. Finally the doctor said: "Right Mr Clarke, as from today you are to take nothing by mouth.

Everything you eat must be taken per rectum".

When he returned the following month he had lost nearly two stones. "Very good Mr Clarke, you've come down to nearly 15 stones but you must lose at least another three. Carry on with your diet and see me in another month. Any problems?"

"No doctor, I am feeling fine".

As the patient walked towards the door, the doctor noticed he was walking in a peculiar manner.

"Mr Clarke is there anything wrong with your legs".

"No doctor they are fine".

"Then why are you walking with a peculiar waddling gait?"

"I am only chewing some bubble gum doctor!"

A man entered a crowded restaurant and was obliged to share a table with a stranger. The man ordered his dinner, a juicy steak, and when it was served he burrowed into his pockets looking for something.

Looking at the stranger he exclaimed "Oh! dear, I have forgotten by dentures".

To his surprise the stranger dived into his bag and produced a set of dentures and said "Let me help you, try these".

The man tried them but they did not fit too well, so the stranger produced another set and then another which fitted perfectly.

"Doctor", said the man, "I have always been troubled with my dentures, but this set fit me perfectly.

"May I have your name and address as I would like to consult you professionally".

The stranger sadly shook his head, "I am not a doctor, I am an undertaker".

*   *   *

Overheard in a Private doctor's clinic. . .

Young Doctor: "Why do you always ask your patients what they have for dinner?"

Old Doctor: "It's a most important question, for according to their menus I make out my bills".

How does a man know when he is getting younger?
When he gets up for a rest instead of going to bed.

*   *   *

The famous prima ballerina went to see a Harley Street specialist.

"Doctor, I've got a very embarrassing problem. I am alright while I am dancing but when I twist round, I break wind. It doesn't smell but it is very embarrassing".

"Can you give me a demonstration, Miss?"

She then started to dance her routine and as she was doing the twist she let one out right under the doctor's nose.

"You see what I mean doctor, it doesn't smell but it is embarrassing".

"I will give you some tablets for the wind but I'm afraid you will have to have an operation on your nose".

"On my nose doctor, why?"

"Because young lady, it stinks like hell!"

How does a man know when he is getting old?
When it takes him all night to do what used to do all night.

* * *

CHINESE PROVERB:
VIRGINITY like bubble . . . One PRICK all gone.

* * *

There was a man who had a "W" tatooed on each buttock so he went to see the doctor.

The doctor decided he'd better have a look. The man dropped his trousers and bent over.

"Further" said the doctor, "I can't see".

The man bent a little further.

"Further" said the doctor, "I still can't see".

The man bent over as far as he could.

"W O W" said the doctor.

Did you hear about the gynaecologist who was so clever that he wall-papered his hall through the letterbox?

*   *   *

"IT'S WHAT THE PRESCRIPTION SAID"

A chap went to a party and met a beautiful brunette who seemed very willing! She invited him upstairs to one of the empty rooms, whereupon they both stripped off. But before the chap had slipped off his remaining sock the girl informed him that she had been to the doctor and was told she had VD or TB — she couldn't remember which.

The man was so rampant that he decided to call the girl's doctor, but he couldn't remember the problem either.

"I had two girls in my surgery today", said the doctor, "one had VD and the other had TB".

"What should I do?" pleaded the man.

"Chase her round the room a few times", suggested the doctor, "and if she coughs, go ahead and make love".

*   *   *

"Doctor! Doctor! I keep thinking I'm a kangaroo".

"Nonsense — just hop off home and take these tablets — and mind your tale as you go out".

A young man who was about to enter Medical College told his father he had decided to specialise in Obstetrics.

"What do you want to do that for?" enquired his father.

"By the time you graduate some other doctor would have found a cure for it".

*　　　　*　　　　*

Joan: "Did you hear Erica is marrying her X-ray Specialist?"

Jane: "Well she's lucky. Nobody else could ever see anything in her".

*　　　　*　　　　*

"I think you ought to stop taking sleeping pills every night", the doctor told the famous star.

"They are habit forming".

"Habit forming!" replied the star.

"Don't be absurd, I have been taking them for twenty years".

Half the people in this world are crazy and the other half is driving the other half crazy.

*   *   *

"FANCY MEETING **YOU** HERE!"

A young man from Yorkshire was called up to join the army. He didn't want to but he had no choice. So, when he went to the doctor for his medical examination he complained of various aches and pains in the hope that the doctor will fail him on medical grounds.

The doctor examined him and found him physically and mentally fit. He told the lad: "I am pleased to tell you that you are in perfect health. In fact Her Majesty's forces would be proud to have a young man like you. However, there is one more thing before we complete your medical report. Give me a specimen of your urine in this bottle and then *you are in the army*". The lad said: "I have just been to the toilet doctor". The doctor told him to take the bottle and go back in the waiting room.

"When you have passed some water leave it with my receptionist and come back next week for the results". The young man took the bottle and ran home as fast as he could. His dad was leaving for the pub when he reached home. "Dad! Dad! before you go to the pub can you pass some water in this bottle".

He told his mother: "Mum, before you go to the bingo can you pass some water in this".

His sister was getting ready to go out with her boyfriend. He asked her too to pass some urine into the same bottle, filled it up with his own, shook it up well and took it back to the reception.

The following week when he went back for the results, the doctor was somewhat puzzled by the laboratory report.

"There is something very strange about this report. I shall have to consult my colleagues regarding this. If you go back in the waiting room I shall call you when I've sorted it out".

Some twenty minutes later he was called back into the doctor's room. "This report shows that your Dad has got gonorrhoea, your Mum's on the change, your sister is pregnant and *you are in the army!*"

Once upon a time, there was a beautiful nurse whose name was Virginia.
She was called Virgin for short . . . but not for long!

*   *   *

"Doctor, doctor! I feel like a snooker ball".
"Get to the end of the cue".

*   *   *

"Doctor, doctor! I feel like a cup of tea".
"Sit down and don't stir".

The doctor's phone rang in the middle of the night.

"Hello, Is that the doctor? — This is Mrs Cook speaking".

"Hello, Mary, what is wrong? Is it your chest again, or is it your husband's?"

"No doctor, we are both quite well".

"Then what is your problem?"

"Doctor, it is my dog. It has got coupled with my next door neighbours' bitch, on our front lawn. They are disturbing all the neighbours. We've done everything we can think of to separate them. Can you suggest something?"

"Have you tried pouring a bucket of water on them?"

"We've done that, doctor".

"Have you tried hitting them with a broomstick in the middle?"

"We've tried that as well, doctor. Nothing has worked".

"Alright, Mary, is your telephone cord long enough to reach the front lawn?"

"Yes, doctor".

"Can you take the telephone and put it down on the lawn beside the dogs. I'll ring back in a couple of minutes".

"Why, doctor, do you think it will work?"

"Well, I can't be sure, but it certainly DID WORK, for ME a few minutes ago!"

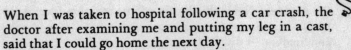

When I was taken to hospital following a car crash, the doctor after examining me and putting my leg in a cast, said that I could go home the next day.

In the morning, however, he announced, "I think you'd better stay another day to see if something new turns up. I did not know how badly you were smashed up until I read about the accident in the newspaper".

*　　　*　　　*

The Health Minister, visiting a mental hospital had difficulty getting the telephone connection to London.

Exasperated he shouted to the operator, "Young Lady, do you know who I am?"

"No", was the calm reply, "but I do know where you are".

*　　　*　　　*

He: "Do you know the difference between Ammonia and Pneumonia".

She: "Yeah, one comes in bottles and the other in chests".

1st medico: "Did she blush when her shoulder strap broke?"

2nd medico: "I didn't notice".

*   *   *

A middle aged man consulted his doctor regarding his stammering.

He was finally referred to a Harley Street specialist who removed an inch off his organ which cured his stammer.

Two months later the patient went back to see the surgeon:

"Doctor, my wife wants me to have the operation reversed. Do you think it is possible?"

"N-n-n-o-tt B-b-b-l-o-o-d-y L-l-l-l-i-k-e-l-y", replied the surgeon.

*   *   *

The family doctor was visiting the old lady whose husband had died while he was on holiday. "I am sorry to hear about Joe's passing away.

He was such a nice old man that he must be in HEAVEN by now. It is a pity we will never see him again".

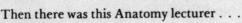

Then there was this Anatomy lecturer . . .

"Ladies and Gentlemen, last week we were discussing the anatomy of the female genitalia. Does anybody remember where we stopped last time?"

"At the vagina, sir".

"That's right, miss. Last week we stopped at the vagina — today we'll go into it".

*　　　　*　　　　*

Patient to Psychiatrist: "Doctor, I keep thinking I'm a wheelbarrow".

Psychiatrist: "You must not let people push you around".

*　　　　*　　　　*

Newly qualified doctor, examining a patient with bronchitis:

"Can you say 110 please".

Ward sister: "You mean 99 doctor".

Doctor: "No, sister. Since your days, it has gone up due to inflation".

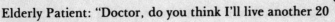

Elderly Patient: "Doctor, do you think I'll live another 20 years?"

Doctor: "Do you drink?"

Patient: "No".

Doctor: "Do you smoke?"

Patient: "Never".

Doctor: "Do you have any sexual activities?"

Patient: "Oh no! Doctor!"

Doctor: "Then what the hell do you want to live another 20 years for?"

*   *   *

The young intern's wife woke him up in the middle of the night:

"Darling, I think there's a burglar downstairs".

The doctor quickly got ready, put his white coat on, and ran downstairs.

Some 2 hours later, he returned.

"Did you catch the burglar?" asked his wife, excitedly.

"What burglar?" he replied: "I've just finished my night rounds!"

A girl in Northern Ireland was expecting triplets. She was shot in the abdomen three times, and was rushed to the hospital. The obstetrician did a Caesarian section and removed the three babies — two girls and one boy — all alive and well.

Later, the obstetrician told the mother — "You and all three babies are all OK. However, I couldn't remove the bullets, because each baby has one lodged in its tummy. But don't worry, they will pass the bullets in their faeces when they grow up.

Some 16 years later, the first girl came rushing to the mother and said: "Mum — I've just passed a bullet in my stools".

It's OK", said the mother "I know all about it".

Two weeks later, the second daughter came rushing to the mother and said: "Mum — I've just passed a bullet in the toilet".

"It's OK", said the mother, "There is nothing to worry about".

Another week later, the son came running to the mother, crying — "Mummy! Mummy! I've done a terrible thing".

"It's alright", said the mother, "I know you've passed a bullet".

"No", said the son, still crying "I was doing a wee and I've shot your dog!"

Receptionist: "The consultant will be able to see you on May 7th".
Patient: "No sooner than that? I could be dead by then".
Receptionist: "Never mind, you can always cancel your appointment".

*　　　　*　　　　*

John saw a small crowd by the roadside, and pulled up in his car to see what it was all about.

He saw a man on the ground, having an epileptic fit.

As he approached the man, an elderly lady pushed him away, saying: "Leave him alone. I have given him all the first aid".

The elderly woman then ran into her house, and came out a few minutes later with a First Aid Hand Book.

She knelt down beside the man having the epileptic fit, and started to turn over the pages.

John tried to feel the man's pulse, but the lady brushed him aside.

"I am sorry to disturb you", he said finally. "Carry on the good work according to the book, and when you come to the part about sending for the doctor . . .

That's ME!"

Gynaecologist to class of medical students:—

If the mini skirt gets any shorter, women will have two more lips to paint, two more cheeks to powder, and a little more hair to comb!

* * *

The doctor's 'phone rang in the middle of the night.

"Doctor! This is Mr Williams of 87 London Road. My wife has terrible pains. Can you come to see her straight away, please. She is in terrible agony. I think she's got appendicitis".

"That's impossible. Your wife had her appendix out last year. Have you ever heard of anyone having a second appendix?"

"No, doctor", said Mr Williams, "but have you ever heard of anyone having a second wife?"

* * *

Some of the greatest followers of the medical profession are Funeral Directors.

"Good morning, doctor how am I?"
"Well, Mr Jones, good news and bad news".
"What's the bad news?"
"Well, I'm afraid we've amputated the wrong leg".
"You've done WHAT? — What's the good news, then?"
"The bad leg is getting better!"

        *   *   *

The old man was complaining to the barmaid about his eyesight.
"I keep seeing white spots and pink butterflies before my eyes".
"Have you seen the doctor?" asked the barmaid.
"No — just spots and butterflies!"

        *   *   *

Ever heard of the midget who got kicked out of a nudist colony — because he was always poking his nose into other people's affairs?

Doctor: "Good morning, Mrs Jones. I've just received the results of your pregnancy test. I've got good news for you".

Patient: "Doctor — I am Miss Jones!"

Doctor: "In that case, Miss Jones, I have bad news for you!"

*   *   *

A man had his fingers cut off both hands in an accident at a saw mill. He was rushed to hospital.

On the operating table, the surgeon turned to the man and said: "Well, Mr Smith, no need to worry, we can do wonders nowadays. What with plastic surgery, we'll have your fingers sewn on in a jiffy. You did bring your fingers with you, didn't you?"

"No! — I couldn't pick them up!"

"MAKE A JOKE OF IT AND CHANGE YOUR NAME TO PARKER!"

A juryman objected to being sworn-in for jury services, stating that his wife was going to conceive that day.

The judge, raising his eyebrows, said: "I think you mean your wife is going to be confined this day. Anyway, it does not really matter which of us is correct — I agree that you should be there".

*　　　*　　　*

CHINESE PROVERB:
Girl who looks for trouble gets belly full.

*　　　*　　　*

A worried husband consulted the Family Planning Clinic because his wife was having far too many children. The doctor gave him a sheath and assured him that all would be well if he followed the instructions.

A month later, the man went back, saying that his wife was pregnant again.

"Did you follow the instructions?" asked the doctor.

"Well, doctor, it said 'Stretch over the organ before intercourse' but as we didn't have an organ, I stretched it over the piano".

Then there is the cute little story of the male bubble
chasing the female bubble all around the bath.
It seems that he wanted to see her BUST.

*   *   *

"Doctor! Doctor! I keep thinking I'm a pack of playing
cards!"
"Shuffle yourself into that chair, I'll deal with you in a
moment".

*   *   *

The professor asked a girl in his physiology class: "What
part of the human body expands to ten times its normal
size under an emotional impact?"
Blushing, the girl said: "I'd rather not answer that".
On questioning the boy next to her. He promptly replied:
"The pupil of the eye, sir".
The professor turned to the girl and said: "Your
confusion shows. You are not familiar with your work.
You have a wandering mind, and you will be extremely
disappointed".

Student (reading discussion) to Professor:
"Female patient, 35 yrs of age. Chief complaint — married".

*   *   *

A young man went to the doctor and said that he wanted to get married but he was worried about the small size of his member.

The doctor advised him to go and stay on a farm, dip his member in milk several times a day, and get it sucked by a calf.

Some months later, when they met in the street, the doctor asked the fellow — "How's your marriage?"

"Oh, I didn't get married, doctor, I bought the calf instead".

*   *   *

Doctor: "Does it burn when you pass water?"
Patient: "I don't really know, doctor. I have never put a match to it".

The young man, about to become a father for the first time, was nervously pacing outside the labour room.

"This is our first child, doctor", he said to the relaxed obstetrician, as he came out. "How long will we have to wait after the baby is born, before we can . . . resume marital relations?"

"Well, that depends", said the seasoned old doctor, "On whether she is in the ward, or in a private room".

*   *   *

NEW BOOKS
Physiology of Puberty,
                    by I C Morhair

*   *   *

At an Army Medical examination the youthful Medical Officer remarked:— "Ah Yes! — You've been circumcised".

"No Sir! — Just fair wear and tear", replied the giant cockney lad.

CHINESE PROVERB:
She who sits on judges lap gets honourable discharge.

*   *   *

Woman Patient: "I've come to see you about my husband, doctor. We've been married for over 20 years, and he's been a good husband. He was happy and contented and loved me very much. But since he came to see you with his head pains, he's a different man.

"He is never at home, doesn't take me out. Doesn't buy me anything or give me any money. He doesn't even look at me. Your treatment seems to have changed his entire personality".

Doctor: "I didn't give him any treatment at all". "All I did was to give him a note to see the optician and get a pair of glasses".

*   *   *

CHINESE PROVERB:
He who laughs lasts.

CHINESE PROVERB:
Rape impossible, woman with skirt up can run faster
than man with trousers down.

*   *   *

The House Surgeon of a big hospital was attending to the injury of a woman whose arm had been severely bitten.

As he was dressing the wound, he frowned and remarked: "I can't imagine what sort of creature must have bitten you. This is too small for a horse's bite and too large for a dog's".

"Oh, Sir", explained the patient, "it was not an animal at all, it was another lady".

*   *   *

Sign in clinic waiting room.

"Ladies in the Waiting Room will you please not exchange symptoms.

"It gets the Doctors hopelessly confused".

*   *   *

A Lecturer on Migraine: "Migraine is brought about by mental stress, and is often seen in conscientious patients. Hence, if a politician consults you for a headache, NEVER diagnose migraine!"

A pompous surgeon, with an entourage of students, arrived at a patient's bed.

He explained the case, and then asked each in turn whether an operation was indicated.

The brightest student replied first, and gave his opinion that an operation was not indicated.

So, the others took the hint, and all replied likewise.

"You are all wrong", said the great man, "I shall operate tomorrow".

"No you won't", said the patient, getting out of bed, "Ten-to-one is a good enough majority for me — give me my clothes I am going home".

*　　　*　　　*

The young, newly-qualified nurse had written . . .

"2.00 am . . . Mrs Brown's suction machine broke down. Dr Morton informed.

No other sucker available . . ."

The couple set off by train for their honeymoon. All they could get were two upper bunks opposite each other. During the night, the bridegroom woke up and called to the bride — "Darling, come over to my bed".

"I can't", she replied, "I've no way of getting across".

"Look", said the bridegroom, "I've got something long and hard — I'll turn it in your direction — use it to climb over".

"Oh, yes?" came the voice from the lower bunk — "and how the hell do you think she'll get back?"

*　　　　*　　　　*

This professor was famous for his dull and boring lectures. One day, he came to the lecture theatre with a large sticking plaster on his face.

After the lecture, one of the medical students asked him: "Sir, what happened to your face this morning?"

"Ah! You see, when I was shaving this morning, I was thinking about the younger generation of doctors, and concentrating on the lecture so much, that I cut my face".

"Sir, in future, you should concentrate on your face and cut your lecture".

CHINESE PROVERB:
Wise man not give piano to his girlfriend, he give upright organ.

*   *   *

The seventy year old man went to see his GP.
"Doctor, I am getting married to a 26 year old girl next week. Is there any advice that you can give me?"
"Yes", said the doctor, "At your age, in your state of health, I do not think it is good to have sex. So, I'll give you some tablets. Take two tablets every time you want to have sex".
"Before or after?" asked the old man eagerly.
"Instead of", replied the doctor . . .

*   *   *

CHINESE PROVERB:
Puberty is age you beat about the bush.

A cocky young lieutenant was trying to put one over on the elderly army Medical Officer. Having tolerated him for a few minutes he retorted: "Look son, don't try to be smart with me. I was in uniform, when you were in liquid form".

*   *   *

CHINESE PROVERB:
VD is disease in primitive man who wasn't civilised enough to take cover.

*   *   *

A pretty young miss walked up to the druggist and asked — "May I have some talcum powder, please?"
He said — "Yes, M'am, walk right this way". . . . She replied . . . "If I could walk that way, I wouldn't need any talcum powder".

"IT'S THE FLU"

WOMAN . . . An animal which micturates once a day, defaecates once a week, menstruates once a month, procreates once a year, and copulates whenever she gets an opportunity.

*   *   *

She was complaining bitterly to her husband . . .

"How many times have I told you to change our doctor.

He is so old and deaf he should be in a geriatric ward himself".

"What has he done this time? Did he make another pass at you darling?" said the husband angrily.

"Oh No! He gave me the wrong tablets again. This is the third time he has tried to kill me".

"Come on, darling! Give him another chance. After all, the rest of your family were all under him until they died".

"YOUR ARTHRITIS HAS COME BACK?
—SO HAS YOUR CHEQUE"

*   *   *

MEDICAL COLLEGE . . . A fountain of knowledge where all go to drink.

A beautiful girl appeared at the gates of heaven and asked to be admitted.

St. Peter asked her the routine question: "Are you a virgin?"

"Of course", she replied.

To make certain, St. Peter instructed one of the Heavenly Gynaecologists to examine her. When he finished, the doctor reported: "I think we can let her in, but there were seven small dents in her hymen".

Old Peter decided he couldn't deny her admittance for such minor defects, so he sent her along to the registration clerk.

"Your name?" asked the clerk.

"Snow White" she replied.

*   *   *

DIFFERENCE BETWEEN FRUSTRATION AND PANIC

Frustration is the first time you discover you can't do it the second time.

Panic is the second time you find out you can't do it the first time.

*   *   *

NEUROTIC . . . A woman who likes a psychiatrist's couch better than a double bed.

A doctor and receptionist went to a conference in London.

They were booked into separate rooms, but they were late.

When they arrived, they were informed that there was only one room available for both of them, with a double bed in it.

They could take it or leave it.

They booked in, because they had no alternative.

In the middle of the night, the receptionist said: "Doctor, it is a bit chilly in here — could you close that window please?"

Doctor said — "Would you like to pretend that you are my wife tonight?"

"Oh Yes! I would love to" she said, with a lot of enthusiasm.

"Then get up and close the bloody window yourself!"

*　　　　*　　　　*

HYPOCHONDRIAC . . . A person who wants to have her ache and treat it too.

The forgetful professor had left his umbrella in his hotel room when checking out. He missed it on the way to the train station and, having time to spare, hurried back. He found the room and was about to ask a passing chambermaid to open it for him, when he became aware of voices within and realised that, in the brief time since his departure, the room had been let to new occupants.

"Whose little baby are you?" asked a youthful male voice from behind the door, and the question was followed by the sound of kisses and a girlish giggle.

"Your little baby", said the youthful female voice.

"And whose little hands are these?" asked the boy.

"Your little hands", responded the girl, with more giggles of delight.

"And whose little knees . . . and whose little —"

"When you get to an umbrella", said the professor, through the door, "It's mine!"

*   *   *

A consultant is a doctor who knows more and more about less and less, until eventually, he knows EVERYTHING about NOTHING.

A general practitioner is a doctor who knows less and less about more and more, until eventually, he knows NOTHING about EVERYTHING.

A man went to his local Health Centre and asked for a new pair of glasses. The clerk looked up the records and said, "You only had the last pair a month ago".

"I know", he said, "but I got them broken in an accident".

"Was it a domestic accident, road accident or an accident at work?" asked the clerk.

"No, it wasn't any of those", said the man.

"What was it then?" snapped the clerk.

"I — I don't like to tell you" stammered the applicant.

"No satisfactory explanation, no new glasses", retorted the clerk.

"Very well then", said the man, "I was kissing my girl".

"How the hell could you break your glasses kissing a girl?"

"You see, she crossed her legs!"

*   *   *

A doctor was running down lawyers and barristers.

"Why are you always so bitter against our profession?", a barrister asked him.

"Well", said the doctor, "you must admit that your profession doesn't exactly make angels of men".

"No", replied the barrister, "You undoubtedly have the advantage of us there, doctor".

Heavy rainfall had flooded from the choked grid, causing a deep pool of water to obstruct the entrance to the surgery.

The GP telephoned the local plumber at 11.30 pm asking him to call round immediately. The plumber, who had just returned from the Master Plumbers annual dinner, said: "I will call in the morning, first thing". "No", said the doctor, "I want you now. My patients calling tomorrow cannot reach the surgery, and if you called me urgently, you would expect me to visit you, even if it was 1.00 am".

"Point taken", said the plumber.

Fifty minutes later, the plumber arrived, in evening dress. Producing a small bottle from his pocket, the plumber extracted two tablets and said "Doctor. I am putting these two tablets into the water. I cannot do more tonight".

"What are they?" asked the doctor.

"Aspirin", said the plumber, . . . "and if it has not gone down by tomorrow morning, give me another ring".

*   *   *

"Mr Brown", said the Medical Registrar, "I am glad to say that we have completed our investigations regarding your illness. However, I am unable to give you a diagnosis as such".

"All your internal organs are diseased to such an extent that all my colleagues are looking forward to your post-mortem".

Shortly after he brought his bride to their new home, he found that she had hung a motto over their bed. It read: —

"I need thee every hour".

The next day, he hung up one of his own, which read: —

"God give me strength".

*   *   *

THE DIFFERENCE BETWEEN WIFE AND MISTRESS . . . night and day.

*   *   *

A member of the faculty in a London Medical College was appointed Honorary Physician to the Queen. He proudly wrote a notice on the blackboard in his classroom:

"Professor Jennings informs his students that he has been appointed Honorary Physician to Her Majesty".

When he returned to the classroom in the afternoon, he found, written below his notice . . .

"GOD SAVE THE QUEEN".

Old man of 80, at the doctors, tells him he's marrying a girl of 20.

Doctor: Why are you doing that?"

Old man: "I want a son and heir. Is there anything I can do?"

Doctor: "Get in a lodger".

Old man returns a few months later . . .

Doctor: "Well, is your wife pregnant?"

Old man: "Yes".

Doctor: "Did you take in a lodger?"

Old man: "Oh aye. She's pregnant an' all".

*　　　*　　　*

Husband: "Can I speak to Dr Wilson, please?"

Doctor: "Yes, speaking".

Husband: "I say, doctor, my wife is sick, and looks quite run down. What's your advice?"

(Husband is connected to an Auto Engineer instructing his mechanic on how to tackle a repair job, and gets this reply) . . .

Auto Engineer: "Draw her water off and give her time to cool.

Take off her jacket and jack her up.

If parts are rusty, apply some grease.

Then take her for a ride.

If performance unsatisfactory, give me a ring and I will come and do it myself".

SEX . . . The most fun you can have without laughing.

*   *   *

OLD AGE . . . A time when a man sees a pretty girl and it arouses his memory instead of his hopes.

*   *   *

A Hollywood Movie Queen, who had been married many times, was to get married once again, and went to her doctor to ask for a facelift. The doctor was not keen on doing it.

"I am sorry, Madam, you have had it done so many times that I do not think you should have it done again".

"Oh, please, doctor. I am getting married again, and he is much younger than me. I must look my best at the wedding".

"Alright, I will do it, but it is definitely the last time".

After the operation, she looked in the mirror.

"That's funny, doctor, I never had a dimple before".

"That is not a dimple, Madam, that is your navel! If I was to lift your face again, you would have to shave!"

A patient in the Mental Hospital was leaning over the wall overlooking the road one day, and he saw a man pushing a wheelbarrow full of manure.

"What's that for?" he asked.

"It's to put on my Rhubarb" replied the man.

"You should come in here. We get custard on ours".

*   *   *

HIGH FIDELITY . . . A drunk who goes home regularly to his wife.

*   *   *

The voluptuous blonde entered the dentist's surgery in an obvious state of agitation.

She sat down in the chair, and fidgeted nervously as the dentist prepared his utensils.

"Oh, doctor", she exclaimed, as he prepared to look into her mouth,

"I'm so afraid of dentists. Why, I think I'd rather have a baby than have a tooth drilled".

"Well, miss", said the dentist impatiently, "better make up your mind before I adjust the chair".

The young man had just returned from the Theatre after an operation for Gall Bladder.

He came round to find the Sister talking to him, and reassuring him that the operation had been a success.

"But Sister", he said, "I can understand bandages round my stomach, but why are my private parts bandaged also?"

"Ah!" said the Sister, "The surgeon who did the operation is world famous and was watched by the medical students. They were so impressed by the surgeon's skill, that they clapped and clapped. So, for an ENCORE, he circumcised you".

*   *   *

ANATOMY . . . Something that everybody has but somehow, it looks better on a girl.

*   *   *

BACHELOR . . . A fellow who can take women or leave them, and prefers to do both.

A lady belonging to the world's oldest profession, went to her doctor feeling quite poorly.

After a thorough examination he looked up from his desk and said: "Now don't worry, I will soon have you BACK ON YOUR BACK!"

*   *   *

MISTRESS . . .Something between a mister and a mattress.

*   *   *

An Englishman, an Arab and an American were conversing on a street corner in Casablanca, when a spectacular oriental beauty walked past them.

The Englishman exclaimed — "By Jove!"

The Arab murmured a reverent — "By Allah!"

Whilst the American breathed softly — "By tomorrow night".

MISTAKES . . . A simple way to gain experience.

*   *   *

A young doctor after the primary FRCS called on the old family doctor.

"In what field do you intend to specialise?" inquired the elder.

"In the diseases of the nose" replied the junior. "For the ear and the throat are too complicated to be combined together with the nose for the purposes of study and treatment".

Thereupon, the elder asked, "Which nostril are you concentrating upon?"

*   *   *

DIET . . . Penalty for exceeding the feed limit.

*   *   *

The tramp asked the pompous consultant to lend him 50p for a cup of tea.

"Neither a lender nor a borrower be",
said the consultant — "Shakespeare".

"Testicles" said the tramp —
"Grays Anatomy!"

Mrs Smith was a lady who was always at the Doctors for her aches and pains.

He kept her going with a prescription and a few words of advice.

But the day came when the prescription didn't work, and poor Mrs Smith died, and was buried in the local churchyard.

She had only been gone two weeks, when her old doctor himself died, and he, too, was buried in the local cemetery, in the next plot to Mrs Smith.

The mourners hadn't been gone long, when he heard a tap — tap — tap — on the side of his coffin.

"Well, *What* is it now, Mrs Smith?" he asked.

"Please, doctor, can you give me something for worms?"

*   *   *

A shapely young nurse was walking down the corridor near the Operating Theatre with part of her bosom showing.

A surgeon who happened to come along ticked her off for improper dress and shameful display of her body.

She corrected the fault at once, and said "I am sorry, Sir, those damned housemen never put anything back in place".

PASSION . . . A feeling you feel when you feel you are going to feel a feeling you have never felt before.

*   *   *

"OH DEAR! AN EMERGENCY AT THE GOLF CLUB — I'LL HAVE TO DASH..."

Some medical students were gathered around a premature baby weighing only 3lbs. One of them remarked about its extremely small size, when the young mother strode up and exclaimed innocently: "Well, what do you expect? I have been married only four months".

*　　　*　　　*

Professor: "A lactating American woman secretes 1,400 ml. of milk per day".
Worried student, to his neighbour: "Thank my stars, I don't drink any American milk food".

*　　　*　　　*

It was a sweltering day in July, and the perspiring obstetric registrar was rushing to examine all the patients before answering a call from the labour room.
"These hot July days are getting you down, doctor", said one woman sympathetically.
"No", said the registrar. "It's not the hot July days that are bothering me — but the cold, rainy nights of the last winter".

A young woman went to her GP for some tablets, because she was having difficulty in sleeping at night since her husband had left her a few weeks earlier.

Her doctor was reluctant to give her any. He said: "These are problems you have to face and overcome. There is no point in taking sleeping tablets. I suggest that you try counting sheep".

"I already have. Last night, I counted up to 298,456".

"Ah! — There you are — You fell asleep after that?"

"No. The alarm went off. It was time to get up".

*　　　　*　　　　*

A buxom blonde of 14 went to her doctor complaining that she had got two lumps on her chest.

The doctor examined her, and said — "That's alright. You are just coming to maturity".

A month later, she came back to the surgery and said — "Doctor — I am worried I have got hairs growing down below".

"That's alright" said the doctor, "It is all part of puberty".

The girl was still anxious, so the doctor dropped his pants to show her.

"Oh! doctor" she said, "When do I get one of those?"

Looking down at the moribund patient, the doctor decided to tell him the truth.

"I feel I should tell you the truth. You are a very sick man. Is there anyone in particular you wish to see?"

"Yes", said the patient feebly.

"Who?" asked the doctor.

"Another doctor", said the patient a little more loudly.

*　　　　　*　　　　　*

A bachelor GP had just returned from a weekend at a stately country home. When asked by a friend what sort of a time he had had, he replied: —

"If the soup had been as warm as the wine, and the wine as old as the chicken, and the chicken as tender as the upstairs maid, and the upstairs maid as willing as the duchess, it would have been perfect".

*　　　　　*　　　　　*

RAPE . . . Assault with a friendly weapon.

A doctor attending the medical dance was talking to a curvaceous young thing in the foyer of the hotel, when his wife popped in. Seeing the beauty, who made a hasty retreat, the wife asked "How do you know her?"

"Just professionally" said hubby.

The wife raised her eyebrows sarcastically and asked — "Yours — or hers —?"

* * *

"If the birth rate keeps on increasing, there will soon be only standing room on the earth, at which time, things should start going down pretty quickly!"

* * *

There was a generous area of disagreement between the sexy young widow and a bachelor friend who had sired the latest addition to her brood. So they took their problem to court.

"Did you sleep with this woman?" asked the judge.

To which our hero replied, sincerely, "Not a wink, your honour. Not a wink".

Psychiatrist to shapely blonde: "Well, Mrs Devalda, I believe you want to discuss a personal problem with me. Take a seat, please, or would you rather do it lying down on the couch?"

"No, doctor, I *can't* do it lying down on the couch".

"Now, young lady, You *have* got a problem".

*   *   *

A census inspector was puzzled to find the child population rate extremely high in a little village, whereas it was quite low in the surrounding villages.

When he questioned a resident of the village about it, the resident replied, "You see, sir, our village is quite close to the tunnel. Every morning at 4.30 am when the first train approaches the tunnel it gives a loud whistle. Well, you see, it is too late to go to sleep again and too early to get out of bed".

There was a young lady of Thrace,
Whose corset grew too tight to lace.
Her mother said "Nelly, —
There's more in your belly
Than ever went in through your face!"

*   *   *

Two drunks were going home one night when they saw a young couple making love in a subway.
"I didn't have sex with my wife before I got married, did you?"
"I can't remember, what was her maiden name".

*   *   *

Clinician: "Why don't women have hair on their chest?"
Medico: "Did you ever see weeds grow on a playing field?"

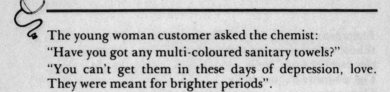

The young woman customer asked the chemist:
"Have you got any multi-coloured sanitary towels?"
"You can't get them in these days of depression, love.
They were meant for brighter periods".

*   *   *

Father, to son getting ready to go out on his first date . . .
"Son, if you are not in bed by 11 o'clock . . . COME
HOME!"

A man paying a visit to a doctor, was surprised to find that she was a woman.

His embarrassment became further acute when she asked him to undress himself for examination.

Her soft hands began the examination, then she paused and said: "Say 99 please".

A warm smile spread slowly over the face of the patient.

"One-two-three-" he continued, as slowly as he could.

*　　　　　*　　　　　*

A man received a telegram informing him that his mother-in-law was gravely ill in hospital.

He went to the phone, called up the physician.

He asked if there was any hope for the poor old lady.

"That, my friend", the doctor answered, "all depends on which way you're hoping!"

She was bragging about her boyfriend:
"My boyfriend has just passed out as a doctor. He is going to practice for a couple of years before we get married".

*　　　　　*　　　　　*

A well known vet was going to the Dublin Horse Show when she found herself in the middle of a traffic jam. She got out of her car and was told that a horse was standing in the middle of the road holding up the traffic. She walked over to the spot where the horse was, to see a well built young lad who, with the help of three other men was trying to move the horse. But it wouldn't budge an inch. She watched this carry on for a few minutes and seeing that they were not having any success walked over to the horse, took off her silk gloves and tickled the horse's testicles with her silk gloves. The horse then ran away as fast as it could.

The young lad who didn't know what had happened, turned towards the vet and said: "I don't know what you did to that horse, but you certainly did the trick. Now can you do the same for me because I've got to catch that bloody horse".

Four medical students shared the same flat. Of the four, only one of them smoked and every morning as he woke he immediately had a coughing fit. The others all warned him that one day he would cough his guts up. But he still continued to smoke.

One night after celebrating the end of exams they all returned to the flat a little worse for wear. "Guts" was particularly bad. The others put him to bed, and they decided to put an end to his smoking. So one of them ran down to the laboratory picked up a handful of intestines and returned, spreading them all over the sleeping smoker.

Next morning the three of them were sitting at the breakfast table when the smoker came down looking very green.

"What is the matter?" asked one of them.

"It's happened", said the smoker.

"What has?"

"I woke up to find that I had coughed my guts up".

"That must have been terrible", said the others.

"It wasn't that so much as shoving them all back in again".

*   *   *

Note from mother to school teacher . . . Little Tom can't come because he hasn't been. I've given him something to make him go, and when he's been, he'll come.

Old time mosquito: "And to think that when I was young I could only bite girls on their hands and faces".

*　　　　*　　　　*

The village undertaker was visiting his gravely ill friend in hospital. "You can always count on me Fred. I'll be the last one to put you down".

*　　　　*　　　　*

A London call girl met a Paris call girl in a pub, and soon they started talking about business.

The London girl was saying . . . "Since this recent war in the Middle East, business is pretty bad. My collection has gone down from 300 to 400 a night to a mere 30 or 40 quid".

"We aren't doing so bad over in Paris. My collection is about 250 per night".

"What do you mean? Stirling or Francs?"

"No — Millilitres. We've gone metric over there".

The foreign doctor was trying to explain to the husband that his wife was infertile, but English words were too much for him.

"Your wife, Sir — she is inconceivable". — Seeing that the husband was puzzled, he continued — "No sorry, I mean that she is impregnable".

To the mounting annoyance of the husband, he said, in desperation, "No, No, — I mean to say that she is unbearable". The angry husband fled!

*   *   *

The young hospital chaplain and his bride had just undressed, and were ready to taste the fruits of love. But before the bride could clamber into the marital bed, he suggested that they kneel down together and pray for strength and guidance.

"Just pray for strength", said the bride, "I'll do the guiding".

*   *   *

CHINESE PROVERB:
Syphilisation is what the west brought to the third world.

Tutor: "Miss, describe the thyroid gland".
Lady Medico: "Sir! It is a midline organ, fairly long, with
two lobes on either side and little . . . No . . . sir . . . er
. . . er.
Tutor: "My god, miss, your mind is wandering."

*   *   *

Shy young man to pretty nurse in Out Patients
Department.
"I can't tell you my problem, it's personal".
After some persuasion, he said: "Alright, if you must
know before I see the doctor, my Johnny is always bent to
one side".
"Don't worry — take off your clothes, and lie down on
this bed. We'll soon have things straightened out".

*   *   *

"Doctor! Doctor! — I keep thinking I'm a pair of
curtains".
"Come, Man. — Pull yourself together!"

A journalist went to interview a famous American Surgeon.

Unfortunately, the surgeon had been called to the hospital for an urgent operation. His five year old son answered the door.

"Dad's in the theatre doing an urgent case. It might turn out to be a simple appendicectomy, or else a laparotomy, or even a cholecystectomy".

"Young man", said the journalist, "have you any idea what appendicectomy, laparotomy and cholecystectomy mean?"

"Oh yea! — An appendicectomy means 400 dollars, a laparotomy 600 dollars, and a cholecystectomy means ONE GRAND!"

*   *   *

Letter from hospital to General Practitioner: —

Dear Doctor,

Your patient, Mr Khan, had a *circumcision* under Mr Raymond Butcher. He made an uneventful recovery and was discharged home today. He will be reviewed in the Out Patient Clinic *shortly*.

     Yours faithfully,
     S P R Scalpel
     (Surgical Registrar)

Patient: "I have difficulty in breathing".
Medico: "When is it worse?"
Patient: "It is worse when I stand up".
So the history read . . . "The patient complains of dyspnoea on erection".

*   *   *

A slightly drunk medico once 'phoned up Dr Wasserman.
"Hello, is that Dr Wasserman?"
"Yes, Wasserman here".
"Are you positive?"

*   *   *

A cute little thing from Bengal.
Wore newspaper to a fancy dress Ball.
The dress caught fire,
And burnt her entire —
Front page, sporting section and all.

It was at that time that Adam had a fight with Eve. He was so annoyed, he took his "leaf" and left.

Exactly one week later, Adam returned. Eve was still angry and said:

"Well, Why did you come back?"

Said Adam: "Oh! My leaf's up".

                    *   *   *

He had joined the army, gone abroad and was fighting to save the Empire. It was rarely that he wrote to his parents.

In his first letter, he said: "Father, I cannot say where I am, but today I shot a bear".

About a month later: "Father, I still cannot say where I am, but today I danced with a beautiful girl".

Exactly three weeks later came the third letter: "Father, now I am in hospital. My doctor says that I ought to have danced with the bear and shot the girl".

                    *   *   *

PSYCHOLOGIST . . . A man who watches everybody else when a beautiful girl enters the room.

Doctor to mother of five sets of twins:
"Do you always have twins?"
"Oh no, doctor. Plenty of times I have nothing".

*   *   *

The bee's a busy little soul,
He doesn't practice birth control;
That's why in happy days like these,
You see so many sons of B's!

*   *   *

Some of the representatives at the recent Family Planning
Conference were: —
Irish Representative: Luke O'Rea.
English Representative: Sir Vical Erosin.
French Representative: La Cont Raception.
Notable Absentee, the Indian Rep: — Mrs Meena Phose.
Cardinal Erectionole, the spokesman for the Vatican is
said to have pulled out at the last moment.

Woman: "I want to see an out-turn".

Nurse: "No, you mean an intern".

Woman: "Oh, well. I want a contamination anyway".

Nurse: "No, no, you mean an examination".

Woman: "Alright, alright, in any case, I want to go to the fraternity ward".

Nurse: "No, no, it's the maternity ward you want".

Woman: "What the hell — out turn, intern; contamination, examination; fraternity, maternity. All I know is that I haven't demonstrated for three months, and I think I'm stagnant".

*   *   *

Then there was the ingenious soldier who obtained leave by explaining that his wife was going to have a baby. On his return, his Captain asked: "Are the mother and baby alright?"

"What baby?"

"The baby you said your wife was going to have".

"Oh, don't be silly sir, it takes nine months".

Lecturer: "Today we are discussing sexual intercourse. There are sixty different ways of achieving sexual intercourse".

Voice from the back: "Sixty five!"

Lecturer: "There are sixty known different ways . . . "

Same voice again: "Sixty five!"

Lecturer: "Despite the gentleman at the back, there are sixty different ways known to the medical profession, the first of which being man on top of woman".

Voice from the back: "Sixty six".

*   *   *

The hospital staff were giving a farewell party to the eminent ENT specialist, who was retiring after many years of loyal service.

As a farewell present, he was given a gold model of an ear. After the presentation, he ended his speech by thanking everybody, etc., and saying: "Finally, I would like to thank you all for the lovely present. When I was a medical student, my father wanted me to follow in his footsteps, and become a surgeon. My mother always wanted me to become a gynaecologist. Today, after all these years, I am glad that I made the right choice".

The 17 year old girl went to see her own doctor because she had not come on for a few months.

The doctor asked: "Any chance you could be pregnant?"

"Oh no! — I am a good girl. I haven't been naughty".

"Allright then, let's have a look at you".

After examining the girl, the doctor asked: "Have you got a boyfriend?"

"Oh, yes".

"What does he do for a living?"

"He is a professional footballer. He plays centre-half for City".

"Very well, then", said the doctor, "you can tell his supporters that he's scored another goal!"

*   *   *

A young woman went to see her doctor with her three week old baby. The doctor prescribed some medicine for the baby's cough and cold, and asked for his name.

The mother said: "Doctor, we haven't given the child a name yet. We don't know what to call him".

Her cheeky friend, (who was with her in the surgery), quipped:

"Doctor, you can write his name down as 'pools' or 'Sweepstakes', because everybody's had a share in it".

An old man came to the surgery saying — "Doctor, my breath comes in short pants".

The young doctor replied: "Surely, Mr Jones, at your age, you don't expect it to come in JEANS!"

*   *   *

An old lady was brought to the casualty with head injuries.

The ambulanceman was explaining to the young pupil nurse that the old lady had received her injuries when she came out of a shop and bumped into a man who was carrying a grandfather clock.

Amazed, the pupil nurse remarked: "Why couldn't the silly man wear a wrist watch like everybody else?"

*   *   *

Then there was this absent minded GP who kissed his car and got on to his wife.

Only the other day, he waved goodbye to the surgery door and slammed his receptionist.

One patient to another who was due to be operated on the following day:

"Do you know why they all wear masks in the operating theatre?"

"Of course! — To keep the germs out".

"Oh no! — They use antiseptics for that. They wear masks just to make sure that you won't be able to say who did it if anything went wrong".

*   *   *

A young man wanted to join the navy. He was accepted, and was told to see the MO for a medical examination.

In his routine questioning, the MO asked the lad — "Can you swim?"

The lad looked at the MO in a startled manner and said — "Why! — You haven't run out of ships have you?"

The well known hypochondriac presented at the doctor's surgery for his usual weekly consultation.

"What's your problem?" asked the doctor.

"Doctor, I don't know what's wrong. I was away last week and haven't had time to read last week's medical journals for the latest developments in medicine".

*　　　　*　　　　*

The barmaid noticed that there was something rather odd about old Joe.

"Excuse me, Joe, I see that every time you have a drink, you shut your eyes whilst drinking it".

"Doctor's orders — He told me never to look at a pint again".

*　　　　*　　　　*

A playboy got married to a famous model. On the night of their wedding the playboy put 3 ten pound notes under her pillow.

She immediately took her handbag and gave him a fiver back.

Jimmy and his baby brother were playing upstairs when their mother heard him cry.

"Jimmy — what are you crying about now?"

"Mum — the baby bit my finger".

"Oh! — It's OK Jimmy, he's teething. He bites everything — he doesn't know it hurts".

A few minutes later, she heard the baby cry.

"Jimmy — why is the baby crying now?"

"It's allright Mum — he knows now".

*   *   *

The absent-minded professor of surgery was on his ward rounds. When he came to Mr Smith's bed, he said to his registrar: "Put him down on the operating list for tomorrow as a laparotomy. It is a very interesting case".

"But sir, he had a laparotomy (exploration of the abdomen) yesterday".

"Oh, my God — I've missed it then".

"No sir, you didn't, said the junior doctor, "You did it yourself".

The elderly family doctor was on his rounds one morning, when he went to a wrong house by mistake. The door of this large Victorian house was open, so the doctor simply walked in.

On entering the large living room, he was amazed to see a group of naked men standing in a circle, and in the centre of the circle was a young beauty wearing a bikini and blindfolded.

He asked one of the men in the circle what was going on, and was told that it was only a party game — sort of blind man's bluff. The girl has to guess the man's name by feeling his body. If she guesses correctly, the man is out.

"Tut! Tut!" said the old doctor, "I am utterly disgusted".

The man said: "I don't know what you're Tut Tutting about, Doctor — Your name's been mentioned three times already, and you are not even at the party!"

*   *   *

The patient had severe stomach pains and phoned his doctor for an appointment. He was given an appointment for three days later. In desperation he went to see the chemist who made up a bottle of white medicine for him. When he eventually got to see the doctor, he showed him the bottle and said that it had done him no good at all. "The chemist told me to take that medicine every four hours and to keep off fats and fried foods".

"Oh! He is well known for his bad advice. What else did he tell you?" said the doctor rather sternly.

"He told me to see you".

Gynaecologist: "What is the advantage of leaving the cervix in a sub-total Hysterectomy?"
Student: "Cosmetic effect, Sir".
Gynaecologist: "They do not look that far".

*   *   *

A GP was describing his new secretary enthusiastically to the family, at dinner.
"She's efficient, personable, clever, punctual, and darned attractive. In short, she's a real doll!"
"A doll?" said his wife.
"A doll!" re-emphasised Tom.
At which point, their five year old daughter, who knew about dolls, asked:
"And does she close her eyes when you lay her down, Daddy?"

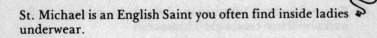

St. Michael is an English Saint you often find inside ladies underwear.

*   *   *

"Doctor I have come with my legs".
"How could you come without them?"

*   *   *

The doctor examining a rash on a patient was baffled and finally asked him: "Have you had this rash before?"
"Yes".
"Ah, well then, you've got it again".

*   *   *

Over a drink, two henpecked GPs were having a rousing battle about the charms of a famous movie star.
"I say she's overrated", said one. "Take away her eyes, her hair, her lips and her figure, and what have you got?"
"My wife", said the other, with a heavy sigh.

Two schoolboys, discussing their housemaster, as he walks by "Here comes old Thrombosis".

Master, overhearing them "What's that you called me?"

Boys, "Old Thrombosis, Sir, but we don't know what it means".

Master, not knowing either, looked it up in the dictionary, and Read:— "THROMBOSIS — A Bloody Clot that upsets the whole system".

*   *   *

A soldier lost his male organ in the war.

He went to the army doctor, who gave him a prescription for a prosthesis. He then went to the chemist, who told him — "You can have a rubber one for £2.00, or a steel one for £3.00". Being short of funds, he bought a rubber one.

Several years later, his son came to him and said — "Daddy, Daddy, the kids at school call me Bouncing Billy".

"Oh! shut up", said the father — "Another quid, and you would have been the Iron Man".

The surgeon, (doing his ward round), said to the patient.
"I've got some good news and some bad news for you.
Which do you want first?"

"Give me the bad news first", replied the patient.

"I have to amputate both your legs", said the surgeon.

"Oh! My God!" said the patient "What's the good news?"

"The man in the next bed wants to buy your slippers".

*   *   *

A man went to the doctor complaining of impotence.
The doctor gave him three tablets: —

"Take one and say — Beep — and when you want to get
it down, say — Beep — Beep".

The man tried this in the surgery, and got a response like
he had never seen before. "Beep — Beep" he said and
down it went.

Thrilled, he went walking home.

On the road, he wanted to try this again, so he took the
second tablet and said — "Beep" — with excellent
results. A car went past — "Beep — Beep" and down
it went!

With only one tablet left, he went home to his wife, who
was wearing a very sexy negligee.

Full of hope, he went to bed with her, took the remaining
tablet, and said — "Beep" . . .

"What's all this Beep — Beep about?" exclaimed the wife!

On the morning following the wedding, the groom arose, walked over to the window and raised the shade.

The day was gloomy, and rain was pouring.

Disgusted, he jumped back into bed.

Next day, it was raining harder.

So he again lowered the shade, and crawled back into bed.

The third day was bright and sunny, and when he raised the shade — he too, went up with it!

*   *   *

An army friend from Yorkshire was told by the Medical Officer that he needed an operation for hernia. He was terrified, never having been in hospital before.

When I visited him after the operation, he was sitting up in bed, and seemed quite well.

"I made a right mess of it", he said. "The nurse put a white gown on me, and I was wheeled into the next room. In the corner was a person in white, sharpening an open razor. As he came towards me I broke out into a sweat, and as he approached the bed, I managed to blurt out in sheer panic and desperation — "Please, doctor, are you not going to numb it first?"

To which he replied, "Don't be foolish, I am only shaving you before the operation".

"Mister, what is the relation of the artery to vein?"

"Lateral, Sir".

"Mister, you have got out of the wrong side of the bed —
Yes, Miss, You . . . "

"Sir, sir postero — lateral".

"I say miss, you also have things reversed. I hope you
didn't get up from the same bed".

*　　　*　　　*

The doctor went to visit the oldest man on his list, who
was celebrating his 103rd birthday.

"I came to wish you Happy Birthday, Mr Smith. You are
in such good shape both physically and mentally that I
don't think I'll need to see you again before your 104th
birthday".

"Doctor, you seem to be pretty confident that I'm going
to live another year".

"Oh Yes! — Not many people die between 103 and 104".

"CAN YOU COME BACK NEXT WEEK?"

Two Army Medical Officers were talking leisurely during the tea break. Senior MO said "Although we go for sex in a big way only 50% is fun and 50% is work."

The junior MO tried to impress his senior. "No sir, I think only 25% is fun and 75% is work."

Just then the medical orderly walked in with a pot of tea for the 2 doctors.

"Private Barnes, what is your idea of sex? How much of it is fun and how much work?"

"100% fun sir!" was his prompt reply.

"Don't be an idiot Barnes! Surely there must be some work involved!"

"Can't be sir, if there was any work involved you would have ordered me to do it."

*   *   *

Dr Korale was writing down a list of Mrs Johnson's problems:
1. Dizziness
2. Insomnia
3. Double vision
4. Headaches
5. Loss of appetite
6. Hot sweats
7. Loss of weight
8. Loss of libido

"How old are you Mrs Johnson?"

"Thirty eight last week".

Dr Korale promptly wrote down:
9. Loss of memory

Diagnosis: "Post menopausal syndrome.

"Doctor, doctor, have you got anything for athlete's feet".
"Yes, a pair of training shoes!"

*   *   *

"Doctor, doctor, I think I have got some wind."
"I've got the very thing for you, here's a kite".

*   *   *

Notice at an army camp:
Troops are warned not to drink any water which has not
been passed by the Medical Officer.

A newly qualified women doctor from Manchester went
to the States on a holiday.

One night she went to a posh night club in Vegas and met
this American millionaire playboy.

After a few drinks the boy suggested: "Honey, let's go to
my flat and have coffee".

The girl knew what she was in for and said:

"I would love to see your flat but not tonight. I am on
my menstrual cycle".

"Oh! Don't worry about your cycle honey.
We can stick it in the boot of my cadillac".

*   *   *

Travel broadens the outlook in a man, and everything in
a woman.

NEW NEWS AT TEN

News is just in that the Saudi's have bought their first
Nuclear Submarine this morning.

Before the ship left Portsmouth, the Royal Navy is
believed to have sent down *four — skin divers to
circumcise it.*

*   *   *

The famous transplant surgeon phoned his butcher to
send him:-

2 joints of bacon

1 shoulder of lamb

3lbs of fillet steak and

2 kidneys

"Two kidneys?" asked the butcher. —

"Doctor — are the kidneys for *eating or transplanting?*"

Police have re-opened their inquiries into the break-in of a herbal medicine shop, which happened 20 years ago. Two Hundred and Seventeen people, aged between 96 and 108, are helping the police with their inquiries.

*   *   *

Lady Arrowsmith-Jones was today admitted to a private Nursing Home in London.

When our reporter asked the Harley Street Specialist who is treating her what she is being treated for, He replied:-

"£200,000."

"No — You misunderstand me. What has she got?"

"Two hundred thousand pounds."

Finally, it was reported in the Soviet Newspaper Tass that the oldest man in the world died today at the age of 138. According to them, the man, who lived in Uzbakistan, was a tee-totaler, a non-smoker, vegetarian and had observed totally celibacy during his entire life, all of which, and his environment away from the decadence of the Western world, is said to have contributed towards his longevity.

Our reporter, Martyn Smythe, went to see his father, who lives in a luxury flat in Mayfair. He was found in his garden, attending to his barbecue, in the company of two young blondes (who are believed to be living with him). In between his Woodbines and his Whisky and soda, he told our reporter that he will be flying to his son's funeral after taking part in tomorrow's fox hunt.

*   *   *

The village doctor bumped into the local 'bobby' on his rounds.

"Good morning doc." said the policeman. "We are looking for a man with a *hearing-aid.*"

"My boy, — don't you think it would be better if you used *field-glasses instead?*"

An elderly doctor and a Presbyterian minister were seated next to each other on the plane. The plane was delayed at the start due to some technical problems.

Just after taking off, the pilot offered his apologies to the passengers and announced that a round of free drinks would be served.

When the charming air-hostess came round with the trolley, the doctor ordered a gin and tonic for himself. The hostess then asked the minister whether he wanted anything:-

He replied—"Oh No!—thank you. I would rather commit adultery than drink alcohol.

The elderly doctor promptly handed back his gin and tonic to the air-hostess, saying . . .

"Madam, — I didn't know there was a choice."

*   *   *

The Magnussons were spending their honeymoon in Malta.

A bell-boy heard the following conversation:-

"Not today, darling — I've got a headache."

"I've started, so I'll finish."

Mum went to the doctor with 3 year old Tommy, for her 28-week Ante natal check. Whilst she was undressing at the doctor's, Tommy noticed she had a swollen tummy.

As soon as they were outside the doctor's surgery, Tommy asked:-

"Mum, why is your tummy swollen?"

"I've got a baby in my tummy".

"Who gave it to you?"

"Your dad".

"How did the baby get there?"

"I swallowed it."

When the dad came home that night, little Tommy asked him:-

"Dad, did you give that baby to Mum?"

"Yes."

"You had better not give her any more — *she swallowed the last one.*"